THIS COLORING BOOK BELONGS TO:

_ _ _ _ _ _ _ _ _ _ _ _ _ _ _

AIRPLANE

BOAT

CATERPILLAR

DOLPHIN

EMU

FROG

GUITAR

HAMMER

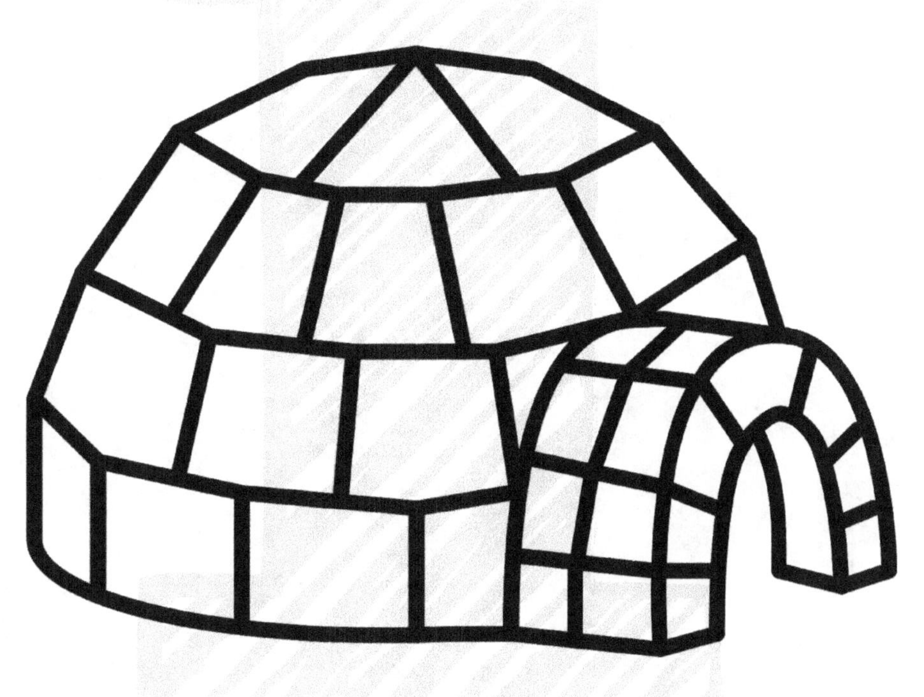

IGLOO

JAGUAR

KOALA

LEMON

MONKEY

NEST

OCTOPUS

PENGUIN

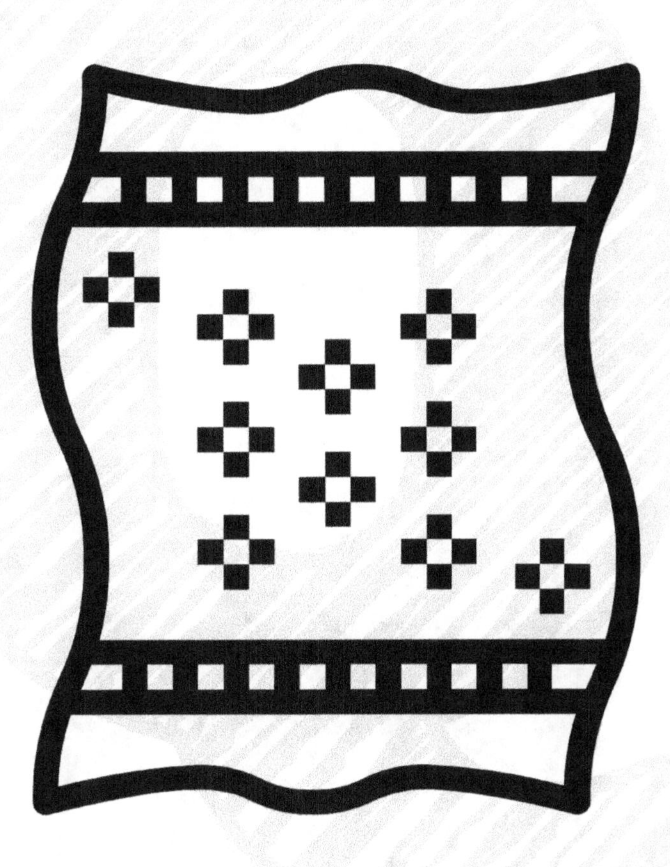

QUILT

ROCKET

SEAHORSE

TURTLE

UNICORN

VIOLIN

WHALE

XYLOPHONE

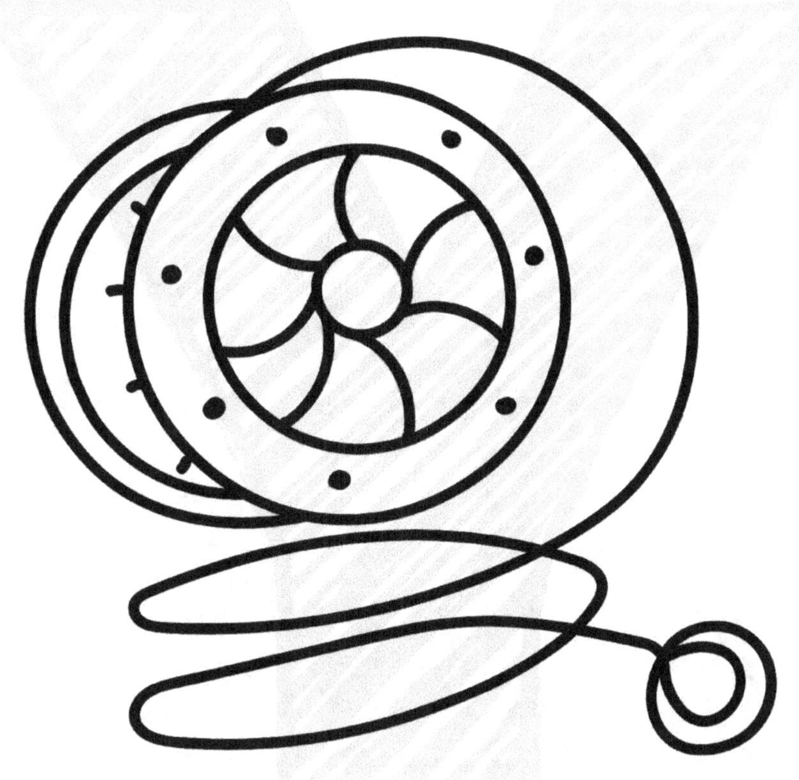

YO-YO

ZEBRA

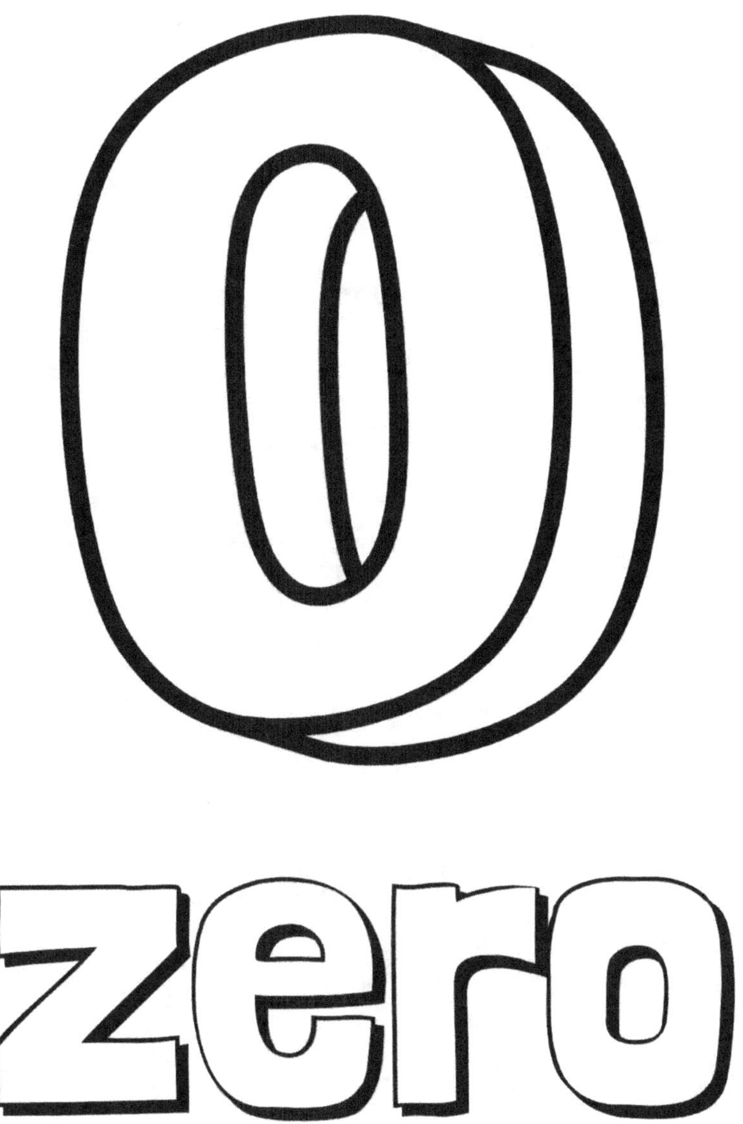
zero

1
one

2
two

3

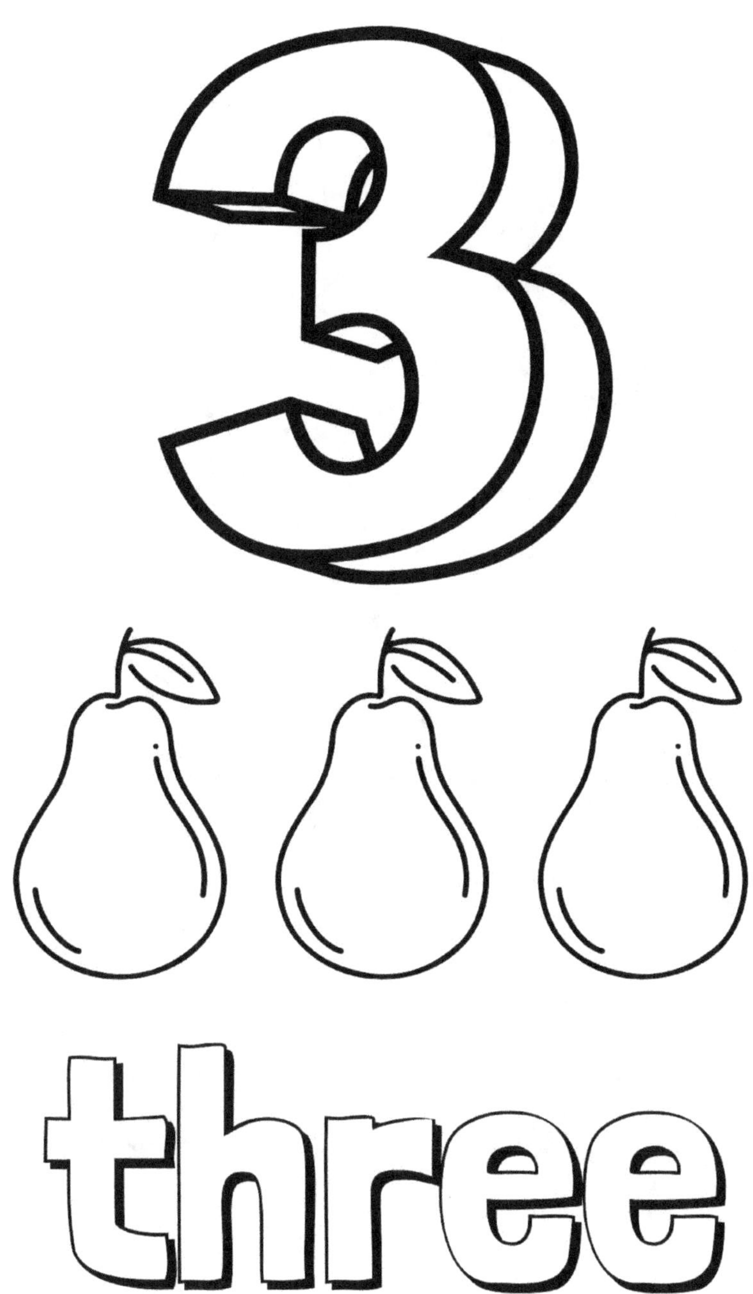

three

4

four

5

five

6

six

7

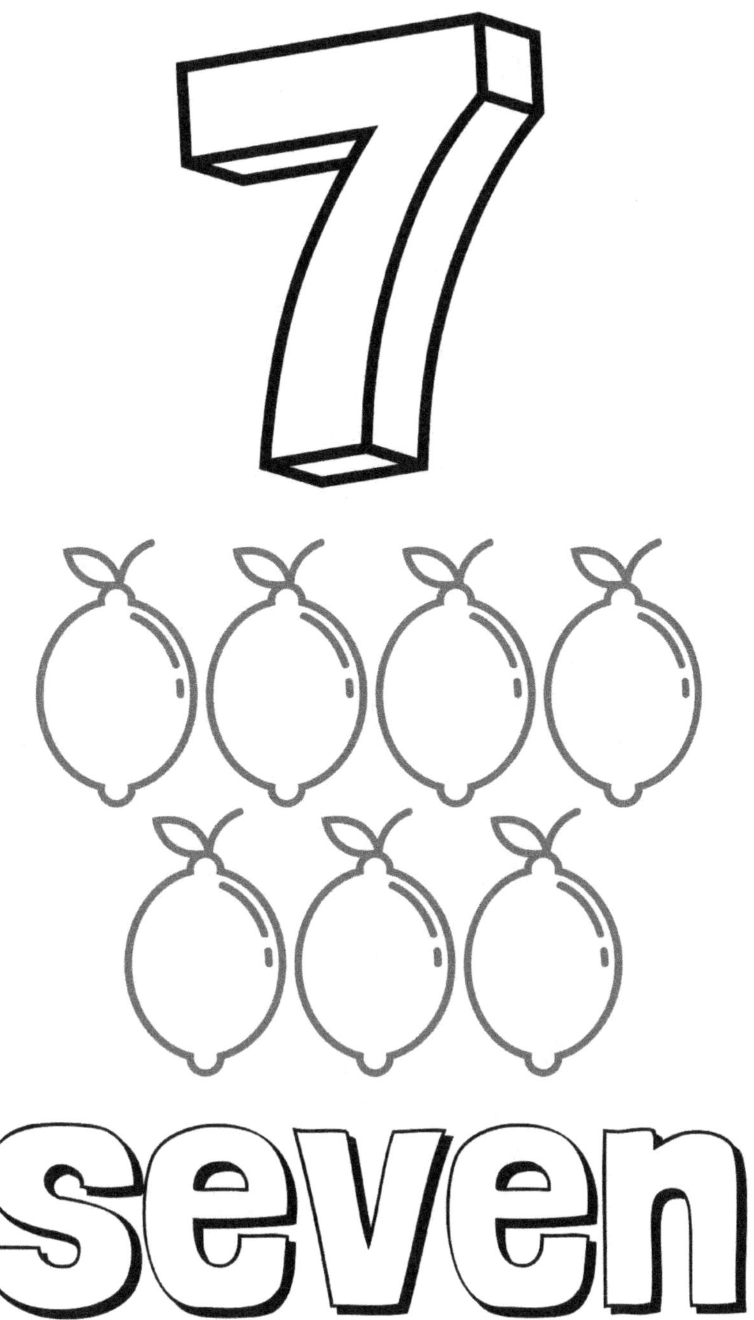

seven

eight

9

nine

10

ten

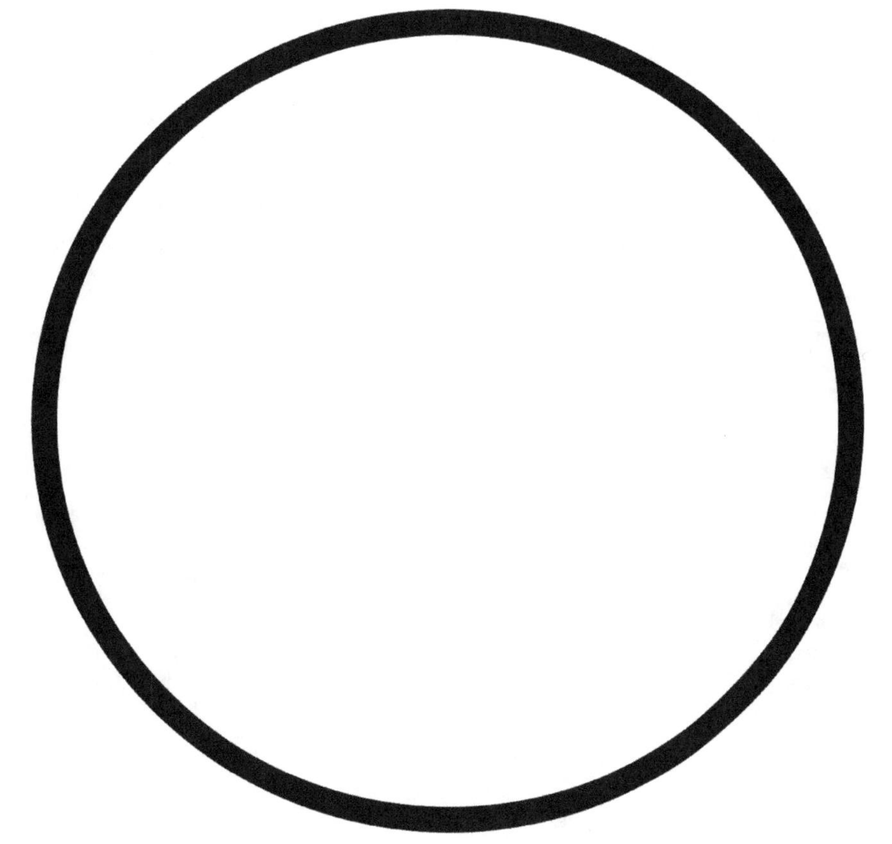

CIRCLE

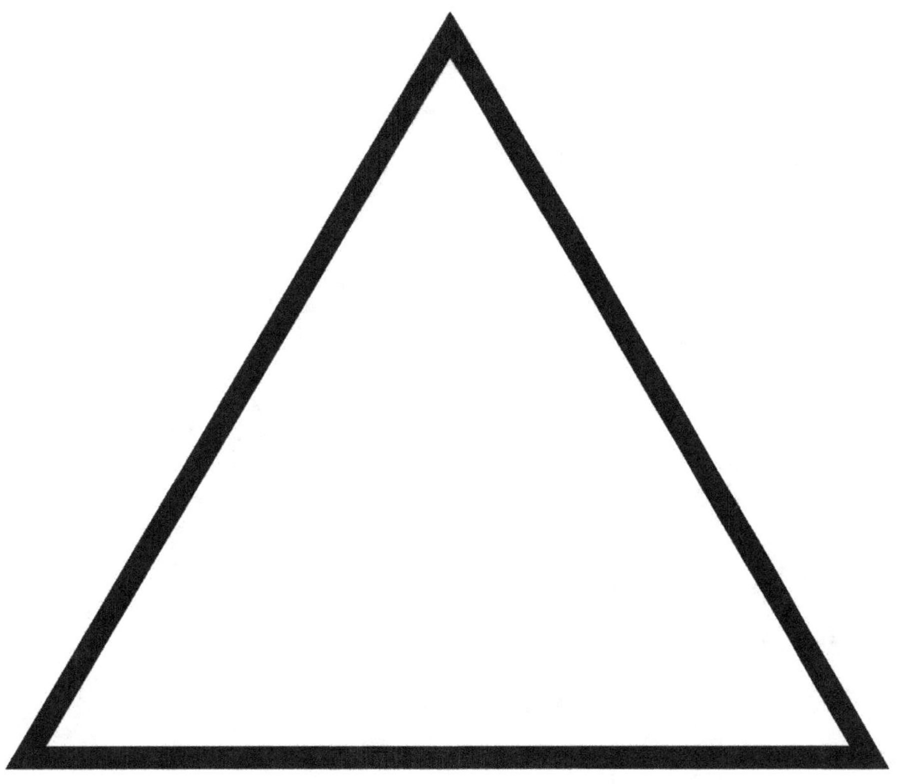

TRIANGLE

SQUARE

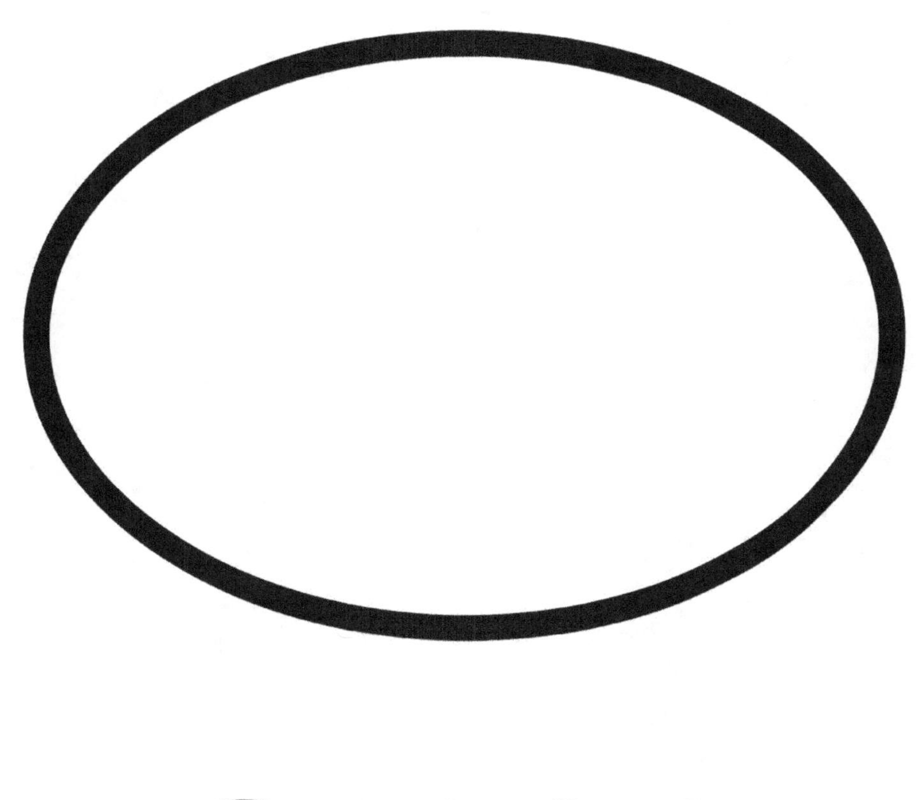

OVAL

RECTANGLE

STAR

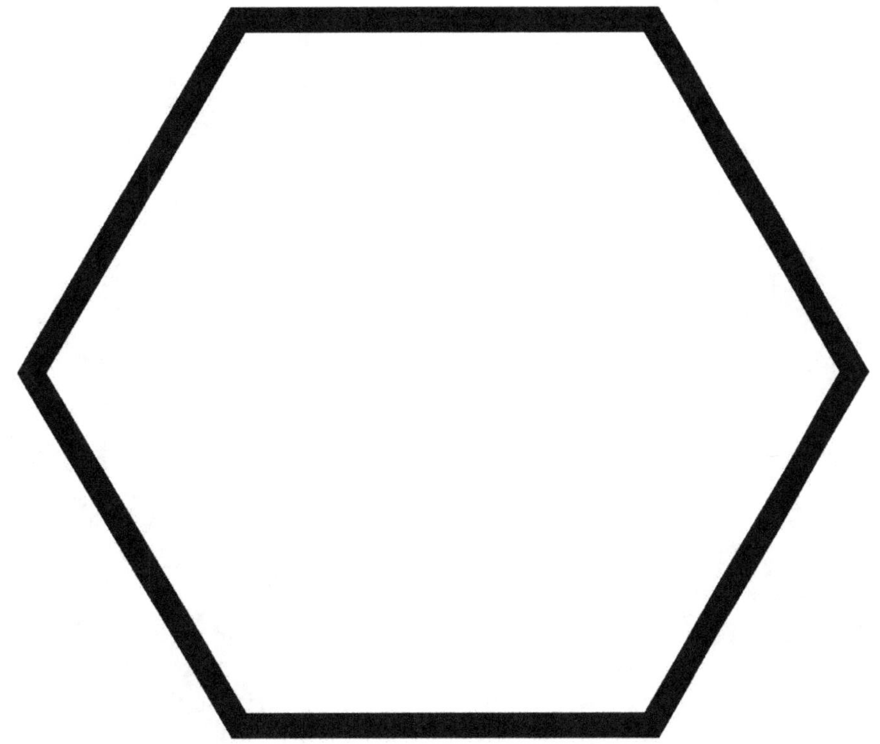

HEXAGON

HEART

OBLONG